FULL MOON

Reflections on Turning Fifty

FULL MOON

Reflections on Turning Fifty

Susan Carol Hauser

PAPIER-MACHE PRESS
WATSONVILLE, CA

00 99 98 97 96   5 4 3 2 1

ISBN: 0-918949-93-9 Hardcover

Cover and interior art © by Barbara Van Arnam
Cover and interior design by Linda Criswell
Text composition by Linda Criswell
Author portrait by Michael DeWitt
Copyediting by Candace Atkins
Proofreading by Erin Lebacqz

Some of these essays are derived from commentaries broadcasted on KCRB Minnesota Public Radio, Bemidji, Minnesota.

The poems "Valentine" and "waxing crescent" are published in *Redpoll on a Broken Branch*, Same Name Press, Grand Rapids, Minnesota, and are reprinted with permission. "Combustion" is published in *I Am Becoming the Woman I've Wanted* (Papier-Mache Press, 1994).

Art credits: "Pink Tulips," 36" x 60", © 1991, p. 3; "Magnolia Moon," 20" x 20", © 1994, p. 7; "Herbal Moon," 28" x 35", © 1995, p. 11; "Summer Solstice," 22" x 28", © 1995, p. 15; "Gnatcatcher Moon," 20" x 23", © 1994, p. 19; "Lotus Bloom," 19" x 19", © 1994, p. 23; "Almond Blossom Night," 36" x 60", © 1995, p. 27; "Red Pears," 19" x 19", © 1994, p. 31; "The Garden," 36" x 60", © 1995, p. 35; "Gardenias," 17" x 17", © 1995, p. 39; "Messenger," 48" x 48", © 1994, p. 43; "Harvest Moon," 23" x 20", © 1994, p. 47; "Moon Rise," 15" x 11-¹/₂", © 1995, p. 51.

Library of Congress Cataloging-in-Publication Data
Hauser, Susan, 1942–
        Full moon: reflections on turning fifty / Susan Carol Hauser.
           p. cm.
        ISBN 0-918949-93-9 (alk. paper)
        1. Hauser, Susan, 1942–. 2. Middle aged woman–United
States–Psychology–Case studies. 3. Middle age–United
States–Psychological aspects–Case studies. 4. Midlife crisis–United
States–Case studies. 5. Birthdays–Psychological aspects–Case studies. I. Title.
HQ1059.5.U5H38 1996
305.24′4–dc20   96–1473
                                                                  CIP

For my sisters,

Gretchen and Karen,

and my brother Nick,

for their constant love;

for Helen Bonner,

Marilyn Heltzer,

and Bea Knodel,

whose comments

helped form this book;

and for Bill, Andrew,

and Debbie, of course.

Contents

Introduction

Human beings love anniversaries. I think in part we like to have an excuse to celebrate and, in part, we like to identify our place in the river of our own lives—to contemplate the past, to evaluate the present, and to conjure the future.

But we also fear anniversaries. They let us know that the river carries us forward whether we want to go or not, and they remind us that our turn in the water is finite.

The fiftieth birthday is especially poignant because it is the first decade marker that offers no comfort when we double it. At thirty, we are only halfway to very late middle age. At forty the odds are pretty good that we're only halfway through our personal journey. But most of us have no expectation of living to be one hundred years old, and we have to admit that hoping for eighty was a stretch.

The day after my forty-ninth birthday I began to think about my fiftieth. How would I feel? What would I fear? What would I hope for? More out of cowardice than courage, I decided I would not let my half-century milepost sneak up on me. I would write myself toward the event, one essay a month for a year, one for each moon. In the end, twelve essays felt a bit too tidy, and I wrote a thirteenth, one for that moon that in some years shows up in the same month as another moon. Sometimes called a blue moon, it reminds us that even the mathematics of the universe is not always neat.

When the year was up, I was used to being fifty. I had learned the tug of the current, and the pull of the tide that, it seems, affects even the river of our blood. On my birthday I celebrated both the accumulation of my years, and the gracious passing of time.

~*Susan Carol Hauser*

FULL MOON

Reflections on Turning Fifty

*Our birthdays tell us
how old we have become.
When we turn fifty,
we have completed our
fiftieth year. Fifty turns
on the horse that is earth,
galloping along its
solar orbit.*

VALENTINE

I was born December 24, 1942. By Valentine's Day 1943 I was seven and one-half weeks old. Not able to crawl. Not able to speak. Not able to call my older sister and brother by name as they peered down at me in my bassinet.

As the count continued toward my first birthday, I did not pay attention to the war that rankled on every front. All I cared about was my mother's breasts. Years later, when I nursed my own babies, my father was pleased. "The dairy bar, your mother called it," he said.

My mother liked having babies. Before I was two, Karen was born, and before I was four, Nicky. With Gretchen and Brooks, that made five under the age of nine. But the year 1943 was mine. I was the newborn, the baby with seal eyes. Brown-eyed Susan, they called me, says my Uncle Joe.

And I was new life in a time of death. We had been in World War II for just over a year. I can imagine sitting in a room in a warm house, hearing news of a war not so far away in the geography of the heart. I can imagine, then, cradling a baby close, lifting her to my face so I could feel her breath on my cheek. I can imagine closing my eyes, and sorrow and joy precipitating into tears.

My mother has been gone, for me, longer than she was here. She died of cancer when I was eighteen. She did not get to contemplate her fiftieth year. She saw two of her children marry, but did not meet their children. She saw the Vietnam War start, but not end. She did not watch on television human beings walking on the moon. She did not imagine the computer that is my pencil and paper.

I am sure she did not count the number of Valentine boxes she had in her life. It is the kind of thing you do when you turn fifty. Fifty birthdays. Fifty winters. Fifty springs and summers and falls. Fifty Valentine boxes.

My mother loved Valentine's Day. We made a box, and she made a heart-shaped cake. And I have heart pans now and I make a heart-shaped cake.
I have eaten from fifty heart-shaped cakes. Fifty times I have seen the sun on February 14th, as it climbs the sky toward the spring equinox, which this year I will witness for the fiftieth time.

For fifty years I have reached for my mother on Valentine's Day. Long before I wrote it, this is the poem I wanted to say:

Valentine

It is February.
The month of hearts.

Blue-
blooded, the sky
throbs with sunshine.

It snows still, yes.
White, white hearts
splash the air,
the eye,
the tongue.

White, white hearts.

Even this far off,
I can hear yours
beating.

The year when Halley's comet came by,
I stood outside at midnight, twenty-five
degrees below zero, planted one eye
against the eyepiece of a telescope and
traveled the sky. I did not see the comet.
I did learn to call by name the constellation
Pegasus and the star Fomalhaut, and to
curse the moon for its brightness.

ANOTHER DAY

Five years ago, my older sister Gretchen turned fifty. My younger sister Karen and I went to spend a few days with her. Gretchen was thinking about death. She did not feel it was imminent but, for the first time, mortality by virtue of age applied to her. Time was running out.

"I'm not going to do it," she said.

"Do what?"

"Die. I'm not going to die."

She was serious. Karen and I did not laugh. To myself I thought, how silly this is, to get upset about a birthday. It's just another day in another year.

But that was five years ago. I was forty-five. This year I am the one who is a half-century old.

Half a century. More than half of a human life span. How much longer will I have? How much longer do I want to have? My body turned the corner a long time ago. I have aches and pains. I get sick easily. It takes forever to get well. The roots of my teeth are dying. I cannot lose weight, and have given up wanting to. If I sit on the floor, I can't get up. If I bend over in the garden to weed my flowers, I get indigestion. One glass of wine makes me loopy. Sugar, an old standby, now makes me sick to my stomach.

Sugar. Mmmmm. But I gave it up seven months ago. To my surprise, my food cravings disappeared. Even more amazing, I do not miss sweets. I eat nuts for dessert, crackers for snacks. Real butter on my morning toast. I lost ten pounds. And I discovered a new joy: I am no longer led around by my belly.

This would not be significant for everyone, but I am a person who planned shopping chores around lunch in town; who wouldn't drive the twenty-five miles to Bagley without packing a snack; who made dessert before making dinner. Food was my infrastructure.

I did not know it, though. I found out last summer at a family reunion. We all stayed at a resort near my town, and every evening gathered, and visited the night away. One time in our cabin, I went to bed before the conversation closed. My room was right off the living area. It was pleasant to lie under the covers with the cool lake breeze coming in through the window, and to listen to the patter of all those people I loved and who loved me.

"Did you go to the hardware store?" That was my cousin.

"The one with the free popcorn?" That was my son. Everyone laughed.

"She locates everything by its relationship to food. We were going to the antique store, and she said, 'It's on the same street as Griffy's, where we had that great soup.'" My son again.

"And on the canoe trip, we ran out of apples, but had plenty of Oreos." My sister.

They went on for a bit, about the trip to town for cake, the place on the way to the Mississippi headwaters that has great pie, the restaurant and chocolate shop in the same building. They weren't being critical. They were telling the truth.

"I can hear you," I called out. More laughter.

Though unwitting, it was essentially an intervention, the kind they pull on alcoholics where they strip away the scrim of cooperation and stand the poor and deserving bugger in front of a horridly clean mirror.

The timing was perfect. I was ready to look at myself. My old struggles were out of the way: I am settled into marriage; the children are gone; my career is in fine fettle. Within a month I quit eating sugar. Now, six months after that, purified, I turn on my heel away from the clutter of my first fifty years, and toward the open canvas of the second half of my personal century.

The moon rises and sets,
fulfilling its celestial circuit
around the earth,
and bringing us news of the sun.

COMBUSTION

I took a sauna once, long ago, in a shed on the shore of a northern lake. I leaned back, closed my eyes, and let the heat come over me. My heart rate picked up. My shoulders slumped. I might as well have been standing in rain, my body awash in water. I was the chicken sort and did not finally dive into the lake, but I did stand out in the night and let the air nibble me dry.

I felt good afterward, lighter and emptied, relieved of the weight of all that sweat that had been lurking inside me. I sat for a long time content to just sit, and then had a good sleep, the kind that comes when you've left one day behind and the next is still in shadow.

That was about twenty-five years ago. I've had a lot of good sleeps since then, but forgot about the beauty of a gratuitous sweat. Forgot about it until a few years ago when my personal female sauna kicked in. Hot flashes. Hormone storms. The fireworks that signal the end of fecundity. A prolonged celebration of the rite of passage that is menopause.

Back on that night of the induced sweat, my younger son Aaron declined to join us. One ladle of water on those benign looking rocks sent him and his five-year-old body fleeing into the safety of the night. He couldn't quite leave us though. He pressed his face against the rough wall and peered at us through a large crack. We could see his one eye, opened wide like a mouth.

When I have a hot flash, part of me feels like Aaron. I watch, astounded, as an invisible hand tosses water on the stones of my body, and I ignite. How can flesh not melt? Then, of necessity, I give up the watch and close my eyes and float on the water, and the fire expends itself. I pick up my little fan and create a breeze something like the ones that frequent northern lakes at night. Then I just sit in the quiet puddle of my flesh.

If it is the middle of the night, I sleep the good sleep of a person cleansed.

Of course, not all of the storms come in the privacy of my home. They come during meetings, during lunch downtown, at the grocery store, or on the street corner while I am in conversation with a passerby friend. Awe strikes the company I keep, their eyes widening as a child's at the scene: my face turning red, water erupting on my brow, my glasses steamed, my arms windmills as I cast off as many layers of clothing as decorum allows, while searching for a tissue to sop the water out of my eye wells.

Yes, I'm all right. Not having a heart attack, just a hot flash, news from the body front: this woman is shedding the garment of the lunar clock. Marvel at it with her, at her luck in carrying within herself an organic sauna. Any time, any place, she may slip away for a few minutes into a wash of free-flowing sweat.

Envy her. It is making her strong. Is tempering her with the fire and water contained whole within her human body.

The sun does not rise and set.
It is we who are in motion,
riding our planet like a carousel
into and out of light.

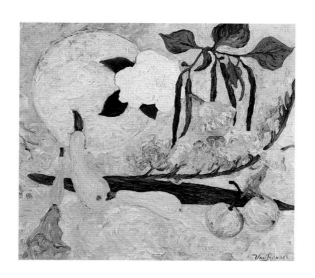

HAPPILY TO BED

When my children were little, I did not think about what they would be like as adults. I was utterly engaged in the day at hand. Sometimes it was a slo-mo movie. I wondered if they would ever grow up, would ever pick up their clothes, wash their hands, or set the table because it needed to be set.

Other times it was a fast-forward flick. Not enough time for playing together, not enough money to go elsewhere, not enough energy to listen long to the stories of the day while tucking their small bodies into beds too big.

But most of the time, we just lived. Got up and fussed our way into the morning; went out into our separate worlds of school and work, and returned in the afternoon, to the privacy of our cave. Talked, made supper, played, went happily to our beds, to our dreams.

That stopped the year Aaron died. He was nine. Andrew was twelve. How old was I? Twenty and twenty-three when they were born. Thirty-three when Aaron rode his bike up through the creek willows and onto the highway, not looking, not thinking. Not hearing or seeing the pickup truck that tossed him out of our life.

Seventeen years ago. Andrew is married now, about to turn thirty, the twenty-year bridge between us always staying the same, while the road back to Aaron gets longer, narrower, less defined.

When my children were little, I did not imagine life without them. Did not imagine getting only one person ready for the day. Did not imagine writing without hiding myself away. Did not wonder what Aaron would be like as a memory. Did not know that every child dies. I am not the girl I was. Andrew is not the boy he was, though sometimes, when he is very tired, or angry, or happy, I can see the child who came to me laughing, or to cry.

When Andrew was little, I did not imagine the comfort of having a grown-up child. When he first moved to California and didn't have a phone, he gave me the numbers of friends and even their parents, so I could find him when I'd had a nightmare and needed to know that he did not go with the car over the cliff.

Once when I was having a bad visit at a friend's, I called him, and the pleasure in his voice at being a ground for his mom, at being the one called because there was trouble, flooded back over the wires, and I floated on the deep water of our long love.

As we did during the day when he was little, Andrew and I live separate lives. But at night, going to sleep in a bed that sometimes seems too big, I think about him, living his story parallel to mine, both of us climbing up to the end of the century, roped together by time.

Aaron said,
"The sky has stars in its mouth."

CHILD'S PLAY

Sometimes I feel as though I am on a familial teeter-totter. Not on one of the ends, but in the middle, astride the fulcrum that does not shift when one end goes up and the other goes down.

The ends of the teeter-totter bracket my life: parents at one extreme, descending; children at the other, in ascension. This image works for me, although my parents have been gone for many years, my mother for more than thirty, my father for seven. Even when I begin to slip along the slivered plank toward their end, I think they will not disappear. They are like the wave that pushes out ahead of me when I walk into water, always staying just a little in front, never moving ahead of its own volition, but sometimes seeming to pull me along.

Now I am mixing my metaphors: teeter-totters and waves. When I do that, I know I am uncertain about what I say, that I have not found the sentence that holds all of the other sentences within it, the way an acorn contains an oak tree, or a seed a child. Perhaps it is from the ambivalence of the teeter-totter. I feel the shift in my hips, my pelvis, my shoulders, as my head turns back and forth, watching one end, then the other.

I like thinking about my parents. More and more, I give up the circumstances and sorrow of their passings and dwell on the snippets of moving pictures of them that I keep in my head: Dad coming home from the store on a hot summer afternoon, sitting in his easy chair in the family room, prying off his shoes, peeling off his socks, wiggling his toes, then giving in to the cushions, tilting his head back, and exhaling the smoke of the day in a long, slow breath.

Mother in motion. Downstairs to the laundry room, down the hall to the bedrooms, around the corner into the kitchen. Bending over a basket of clothes, reaching up for a stack of plates. The only time she comes to rest is when she prepares to go out to dinner with Dad. Then, the counter set up for the five kids to make their own meals, she sits at the big, round kitchen table and paints her fingernails. For the only time in the day, she is not in a hurry. She dips the brush into the pot of color, holds out one hand and draws the brush over and over from the quick of the nail to the tip, the polish flowing in a little wave just ahead of the bristles.

I knew the wave image would resurface. The wave that is my parents, leading me into deeper water; the wave of color flowing ahead of the brush. This is the way it is: The past is not behind us, but ahead, that which goes before, and we follow. The future is not ahead of us, but behind, and will come along.

I shift my weight and turn to my son Andrew and his wife, Debbie. How shall I draw this picture? Do I ride on the crest of the color from their brush, or are they pulled along by the tide of my writing?

Parents on one side, children on the other. I square my feet on the plank and, briefly, bring the teeter-totter into balance.

Star light, star bright,
First star I see tonight,
I wish I may, I wish I might
Have the wish I wish tonight.

FAT CHANCE

When I was twenty I was a slender woman. At five feet six and one-half inches tall, I weighed one-thirty, give or take five pounds. When I was about thirty, I took some of my clothes to a rummage sale. A friend and I were straightening the tables and she picked up a mini-dress, a slim hank of white cloth with spaghetti straps. "Who do you suppose wore this tiny thing?" she mused. I looked at it. It was tiny. Straight lined, no flares, no pleats, no elastic waist.

"I did," I said. She looked at me, and we both looked at the gown she had draped admiringly over her arm. I weighed one-fifty or sixty by then and had given up dresses in favor of slacks, and waistlines in favor of flowing tops.

"You were thin," she said.

"Oh, I don't think so," I answered. "I've never been thin."

"Look at it," she said, holding it up. I looked at it, then she put the dress back on the table. We continued silently at our task, but I kept thinking about that wisp of a garment. I really was thin once, and I didn't know it. I weighed a scant one hundred and thirty pounds, and I thought I was fat. I worried about my eating. I felt guilty when I ate jelly doughnuts. I once ate half a dozen so I could throw away the package and no one would know I had eaten three.

As I sorted through other people's clothes, I tried to blame my self-deception on everyone, anyone else. Twiggy. Family who said, "You're having another?" My parents' friends who said, "You're just large boned," when I weighed one-thirty but was not yet five-six-and-a-half. But I was the one who listened, and didn't listen. I remembered store clerks who said, "You look wonderful," and my obstetrician who tried to tell me I was not fat.

I had an epiphany at that rummage sale: I had been thin once, and I missed it. I began to wonder what else I had missed, and then to wonder what I was currently missing. I could hear myself saying, in response to a compliment, "Oh, you're just saying that," or thinking to myself, "Oh, yeah, fat chance."

Fat chance. I decided then to not miss another minute of my own life. Gradually, I learned to say "thank you" when someone complimented me and, when I doubted them, to stop and consider that they might be right.

And this year I am offering myself a special challenge: to enjoy my body the way it is; to let go of the way it could be, or should be, and to revel in the ship that carries my soul so ably about the earth.

I weigh one hundred and seventy-eight pounds. I work out, and have discovered classy clothes catalogs for "large boned women," so some people don't believe how much I weigh. "You don't look it," they say, the way they say, "You don't look fifty years old." And they mean it. But I want to say to them and to myself, "Yes, I do look it. This is what one-seventy-eight looks like. And this is what fifty years old looks like."

Recently, I have taken to standing nude in front of the mirror. "Look at that belly," I say to myself. "That is the belly of a woman who has borne two children and who loves good bread. Look at the curve of those hips, and the heft of those breasts. That is the flesh of a woman who has lived for half of a century."

The woman in the mirror straightens her shoulders, not missing a thing.

To find Polaris, the North Star,
find the Big Dipper.
Follow north five times
the length of the two
stars of the right-hand side
of the bowl to the end of
the handle of the Little Dipper.
From that small light,
it seems, the universe swings.

CONSTELLATION

My big sister Gretchen, my little sister Karen, and I pull ourselves out of the car, stand upright in a stranger's driveway, and shake ourselves loose. Knees and hips locked into place, we murmur pleasure at the old pines that sway over this house in the woods, and squint our eyes as we move from the morning sun into the cool of yet another garage.

Today, the third day of Karen and Gretchen's visit, we are doing rummage sales. We follow balloons and arrows down county highways and along gravel roads, reminiscing already about the two days just past, and making plans still for the one day left to us. After that they will return to their own habitats, and for a long while every time I pass a place we went together, I will hear their voices.

It is six months before my birthday on Christmas Eve. My sisters won't come then, the season too much to manage, but they are here now. We drive on to other sales, spending our money on each other and loading up the car with other people's histories: a tea set, a muffin tin, a pine cone Christmas tree; three tiny plastic dolls whose eyes open and shut, looking and not looking.

Besides the garage sales, we have waded across the headwaters of the Mississippi River, eaten Ojibwa fry bread at the county fair, and walked down the road that leads to and from my country home. And last night we sat in the yard. The sun went down and loons laughed with us as I opened presents: coffee mugs, a wooden box, postcards, warm socks, tea.

We talked. Gretchen is halfway to her sixtieth birthday; Karen is following me to fifty. If we help each other cross over the marker of each decade, we will have to meet every few years. Will have to leave our husbands and our homes, our jobs and our children. Will be forced by faith to journey to the land of the sister in passage, there to free-fall into the moment, water that carries us out of the past, and into the future.

Contemplation made us unafraid. We even dared to wonder who would die first, but passed the honor on to our brothers. Then, released from mortality, we laid ourselves out on the darkening grass and, touching hands, scanned the sky for the constellation Pleiades, sister stars, configured for eternity.

Red sky at night,
sailors delight.
Red sky in morning,
sailors take warning.

GRACE TIME

If I were an artist, I would paint this picture: my husband sitting on a small folding chair in the middle of our country driveway, halfway between the road and home. He is wearing grey sweats, and is sitting forward a little, knees apart, one hand over the other on the rounded, club top of the carved diamond willow cane planted between his feet. While he catches his breath, I walk on to the mailbox and collect the day's offerings. He watches me stroll back to him, and then we return to the house, me with the chair under one arm.

It is only two months since he turned himself over to the art of medicine. Practitioners opened one leg and heisted a vein. They opened his chest and his heart, and patched in pieces of the good vessel where old ones failed. A week later, when an ulcer blew a hole in his belly, they went back in the middle of the night and darned his viscera. When he didn't die, I said to the doctors, "That's what comes of splitting thirteen cords of wood for winter when you are seventy-seven years old."

True, Bill is twenty-seven years older than I am, in calendar years. But the first time my sister Karen met him, more than twenty years ago, she said, "At last you've found someone your own age." She was referring to my adolescence, when I was called old at best, lazy at worst. Both accusations were a bit accurate, though that did not keep me from trying to abuse my older brother when he sat at the table and spun the condiment tray in the middle and sang not quite under his breath, "Lazy Susan, lazy Susan."

It is with satisfaction that I think back now and shine the light of new knowledge on old behaviors. I have mitral valve prolapse, a congenitally floppy heart valve. That is why in the winter when we went out to skate under the stars and to listen to the lake ice crack, I was the first to hobble, on my blades, back into the house. That is why I sat with Mother at the rest stop benches on the long climb back up from the foot of Minnehaha Falls. That is why as I got older, I came to hate stairways, and to overcome my distrust of elevators.

That is why after Aaron died, my heart leaped into palpitations and tachycardia at will. It took years to untangle the fears, to reclaim stasis. Beta blockers helped for a while, to remind my heart of how it should behave. Then I went solo, at night sleeping with my ear to Bill's back, pacing my pulse to his.

It was good training. As I approach the age Bill was when we met, my tyrant body roars again, and to appease it , I alter my life. I sleep later in the morning, rest more in the afternoon. It makes me mad to have to do it, but then I listen to myself talking to a friend who is eighty. She wants to find a way to regain the stamina she had when she was sixty. "Forget it," I tell her. "The task before you is to use what you have to move forward. You are wasting energy by trying to go back."

Yesterday Bill and I went out to kill the moles encroaching on our yard. I probed around the little dirt mountains and found the tunnels between them. He used the spade to open slots in the earth, and we teased poison peanuts into the passages and replaced the sod. We did this three times, then, holding hands, dragging the shovel, our breathing heavy in the wet, summer air, returned to the house, sat at the kitchen table, and waited. In a while we felt better and went out and did it again.

Today we walked out to the perennial bed we've abandoned. In just two summers the rhubarb has given way to wild sage. Thistles replace raspberry canes and yield to the weight of goldfinches that whistle while they graze.

Beneath our feet, patient in the dark earth, moles wait.

Waxing crescent

quarter moon

gibbous

full

and back to gibbous

quarter

crescent waning

looms

BREAD AND WORDS

"The faster I go, the behinder I get." That's what my dad used to say when I was a kid. I understand it now better than I did then, but for me it is not so much that there are things I must do. It is that I am no longer able to do everything I want to do.

I am constrained in part by a recalcitrant body, and now, in addition, there is so much that I am good at doing. I keep learning new things, and want to do the old things as well. On Saturday mornings I stand in the kitchen and look longingly at my food processor and imagine loaves of warm bread cooling under a clean, white cloth. And then I imagine in their place a piece of paper with a fresh poem left for my husband to discover, and I take my tea and go up to my office, and instead of working with yeast and flour, I work with ink and words.

That is not the only hard choice. Even harder is the winnowing of projects, of committees to join, boards to stay on, good deeds to do. About every three years I find myself overwhelmed, and resign from every organization I belong to. The quiet lasts about one month. Then I let myself be pulled back into the stream of activity that keeps the land watered and lets me feel loved at the same time.

Bread or words; solitude or society. They are still not the most difficult choices. Those come with people. Potential new friends appear on the horizon with the consistency of birds coming to dine at our feeders. I would love to take a walk with this one; to lunch with another; would like to ask that couple to dinner, to learn their life while touching my foot to my husband's under the table.

But the more friends I have, the less time I have for my friends. The more I weed my garden, the less time I have to cut and arrange my flowers.

The more I read, the less time I have to write. The law of perversity, one friend calls it.

It makes me long for old age. I don't mean the old age of just after retirement, when you wonder how you ever had time to work. I mean later old age, when the body says, "Enough. Let me sit." That is when we finally have the time we have always yearned for. Time to sit and stare. To reminisce. To contemplate. Time to be bored. I haven't been bored since I was a teenager.

Sometimes I imagine myself living in an old-fashioned nursing home where I could let my mind wander. My grandmother did that. She became a philosopher, dwelling on the meaning of her day, of the snow outside, of the woman in the next bed. She did not have to do laundry. She could take her meals by her window, or down in the dining room. In the middle of the night if she was afraid, she could tug on a cord and someone would come.

I worked in a nursing home in an earlier life. I know there are injustices and hardships there. But I imagine having profound thoughts and not being driven to write them down or take them to a meeting. I imagine letting ideas come and go like clouds, smiling at them as they pass, then closing my eyes and letting them inform my dreams. Imagine not wanting to do everything I think of to do. No responsibility for making dinner, for being on time, for remembering; the rest of my life a meadow to wander in. My only task, to love myself. My only choice, to keep on living.

If I can cup the round
of the moon in my right hand,
it is waxing.
A friend told me this.

RECORD

Growing up, I acknowledged only two seasons: summer and school. Even after I started menstruating, I was not tuned in to monthly cycles. That came later, when I wanted to get pregnant, or to not get pregnant. For years I kept a little notebook and recorded the first and last days of my periods. Even after my tubal ligation, I kept it up. I liked acknowledging the waxing and waning of my personal cycle.

And I liked the cycle itself. The warmth in my womb as the uterus faithfully prepared itself for the possibility of an inhabitant. The gathering of water in my breasts. The aches and sometimes cramps that reminded me of giving birth. The bright menses, a declaration of renewal. The airy emptiness in my belly in the hiatus before ovulation. The little glowing knot in my groin that signaled the fall of ovum toward light.

I was surprised, then, to discover that I did not miss my periods when they stopped, nor do I miss the marking out of the months. There is instead a new pleasure in a calendar that opens up before me like a long prairie. No monthly breaks in the journey toward death. No harking back. The motion is one way: forward, with challenges strewn along the horizon.

Four years postmenopause and my hot flashes continue. When they do stop, I know my body will still have plenty to say. Already I work out to stay alive. Stretch so I can keep on stretching. Walk so I can keep on walking. There is work to do, time to kill, love to gift, love to garner, and love to lose.

Last week Judith, my good friend of twenty years, died. She was forty-five. The breast cancer she lived with for five years finally took her breath away, but I lost her before that. In the last two years we talked to each other less and less. I made her angry, with all my writing, and coming and going, and breathing without effort.

Two weeks before she died, we agreed I would not call again; she would call me. I knew she would not. For several months, the longing and effort to connect had come from others. Her reach was already toward the stars.

Judith brought me back into lunar synch. I used to check my breasts for change, for lumps, for little beads of hungry cells, just after my period. Now I call on a cosmic clock and palpate at the full of the moon, howling in my heart.

When the
new moon
holds the
old moon
in her lap,
the weather
will be fair.

COME OF AGE

During the grand opening of what Minnesotans call the megamall and the rest of the country calls the Mall of America, I happened to be in a taxi on I-494 swooshing by the Cedar Avenue exit ramp. I squinted to get a better look at the largest shopping center in the United States.

"I remember when that was a cornfield," I said to the cabbie. "Oh, no," he replied, "that used to be Metropolitan Stadium."

"Yes," I said, "but before that it was a cornfield."

He leaned toward his rearview mirror, peered back at me, and said nothing. I was silent too, remembering putsy drives in the country with my grandparents when Cedar was a gravel road, and they said, "Remember when this field was a wood?"

I am paying attention when I hear myself talking or acting like my grandparents. A while ago I realized that I drive slowly. Cars queue up behind me on the road to town, waiting for the long stretch by Lake Movil where they can at last get by me and get on with their lives. I don't mind. I don't mind that I slow them down, and I don't mind that they leave me in the dust. I am, after all, come of age. I am more confident about many things, determined about others. Last summer I decided to give up being afraid of flying. I have almost made good on it, and on two other conscious decisions: to let people do things for me, and to be angry when I am angry and not wait until I go ballistic, as the kids would say.

I'd like to take full credit for my new sense of well-being, but with the wisdom of my increasing age, I admit to being shaped not only by my personal history, but by the history of my time. I am feeling strong in part because of our new president. And it is not just because he is a Democrat, but more because he is my age. His war was my war, not the one I read about in schoolbooks. His Vietnam protest was my protest, and for his and my adulthoods, women did not have to break the law and risk their lives to get abortions.

Even if the president had been for the war, and even if he were not pro-choice, I would still feel the power of having my generation in the White House. Some of us were, after all, hippies, progenitors of the environmentalists. The Greening of America has its roots in the Back-to-the-Landers, the communes, and the war protesters who insisted that we can change the way things are. Most of us who participated in those social experiments are now the establishment, and some of us are effecting more change. We understand getting along with others and with the earth: we gave up our tipis, but we recycle.

A lot of people never did like us. We were accused of being unrealistic and, by our parents' definition, we were. They lived through the depression, and were determined that we not know what that was like, so they protected us. To their dismay, they succeeded, and some of us still assume that we all have the right to live well and to be well.

I like to think ahead to the millennium, when I will be in my sixties, and beyond to 2010, 2020, and even 2030. Compared to the total population, there weren't that many flower children, but we got something right; we've been blamed for the values of a whole generation. And now as grand-mothers and grandfathers, and great aunts and great uncles, we are the status quo. If we have the same fifty years in ascension as did the World War II generation, we may overcome.

"*Therefore the moon, the governess of floods,*
Pale in her anger, washes all the air..."

A Midsummer Night's Dream (Titania)
— *William Shakespeare*

REMARKABLE FACTS

I shaved my arms once. Not my pits. My forearms. I was thirteen. I was sitting in the sun with my sisters and some other girls, and they wanted to know when I would start shaving my legs. I said there was no more hair on my legs than on my arms, and I didn't see what was wrong with any of it, and they said, "Ooooo, look at your arms, what are you going to do?" I was so mad and felt so ugly that I went in the house and shaved my arms and came back out and said, "There. I hope you're happy."

They were appalled, but no more so than my aunt was fifteen years later when I showed up in a sundress and unshaved legs. "Your mother would shake you till your teeth fell out," she said.

No, she would not. My mom was the essence of charity. We would have talked about it, so that I knew the consequences for myself. Once I asked her why a girl neighbor always had boys hanging around her, while they ignored me.

"Watch her," Mom said. I did. That girl pandered to those boys. She waited on them, and cooed, and let them wait on her. It made me sick, even then, and I was a long way from hearing about feminism or the women's movement.

That was around 1958. I was in high school. Another friend had an aunt who was a physician. I commented to my Mother on this remarkable fact and Mom said, "Well, she doesn't have children."

Even with the example of Elna Jo's aunt, it never occurred to me to become a doctor. I would be a nurse. That way I could run an orphanage, and have children around me. It was obvious I would not be finding a man.

A distant cousin came to visit. "Paul will be a doctor," we were told. "Oh, Suzie is going to be a nurse."

I did not become a nurse. Or even a French translator, my alternate career track after I bungled chemistry in high school. I got married a few days after my nineteenth birthday. Six months after my mother died. A few weeks after I was kicked out of the university for bad grades. It did not matter. I shaved my legs and my armpits, plucked my eyebrows, and found a man. We would have children.

I did continue in college, through two babies, and even through the divorce, and gradually I became a writer. Poet first, leading with the heart, then prose, led by the determination to write my way through life.

But about once a decade, I wish I were a doctor. I wished it when I was ill, and when my husband was ill. And I wish it still. Just a few years ago I repeated what has become ritual when the urge swells: I got out a college catalog. Looked up "Pre-med." Ignoring financial considerations and physical limitations, I would start with remedial math. Take chemistry. Biology. Physics. Two, maybe three years of intense dedication to overcoming "academic deficiencies," then seven years of hard labor. When I finished I would be sixty, maybe sixty-two, sixty-five.

The calculations always make me glad I became a writer. The thought of all that knowledge makes me weary. But I would like someone to have said, "Suzie is thinking about going into medicine." Would like to have tried it. Would like to understand better the little node in the heart that sparks its beat.

With my telescope,
I can see ringed Jupiter
and its moons,
bright marbles that stay
with it as though by will
as it crosses the sky.

FULL MOON

It is the morning of December twenty-fourth, 1992. Fifty years ago at this time of day my mother probably knew that my birth was imminent. By dinnertime, I would have arrived, seven pounds, thirteen ounces of flesh and spirit. No doubt my mother cried, and maybe my father too, overwhelmed by both the joy of the possible and fear of the inevitable.

It took less time to gestate into that baby than it has taken me to prepare for this birthday. I started more than a year ago, with a trip to Africa, my first fiftieth-year present to myself. There have been many more, though none so grand as the visit with the animals in Kenya. The others include new shirts, a hand-embroidered apron, a frame for a batik print purchased in Nairobi, and an original painting.

The painting was delivered to our house by the artist, so it would not have to ride in the back of our pickup. She carried it in, and together we nudged it around corners and up the stairs to my study, and she cried the whole way, even though she is glad for me to have it. We hung it on the south wall between the windows that overlook the swamp, and now when I write I have another view, one that makes me feel like I am at the ocean, though the picture is not of an ocean.

I told my husband that the painting was my last fiftieth birthday present to myself, and I think it is, but I did not tell him that the celebration of my sixth decade on planet Earth begins tomorrow. He'll like it, I think. I plan to continue the self-consciousness of my journey toward this birthday, with one variation: I am going to be especially aware of how I spend time. I am going to keep saying to myself, "Is this what you want to do today?"

It will take more effort than purchasing self-gifts because I already feel that I do pretty much as I want to. But maybe I let myself want mostly that which is easy, or familiar, or what seems possible in some reasonable way. Did I, after all, have to wait thirty years to go to Africa? Once I decided to do it, it only took me two years to get there. And now I've used up my one energizing dream. Where on earth do I want to go when I am sixty?

I didn't realize I had such slender expectations for myself. I have a lot of conjuring to do, and only ten years to get it done, and there will be other decades after that. I'm going to start casting little magnet desires out ahead of me. A trip to Australia; a pilgrimage down the Mississippi from head to toe; a long walk on the Appalachian Trail; a screened porch off the kitchen: possibilities that will pull me toward them the way the sun pulls us out of bed in the morning, and sunset pulls us back home at night.

I know why the artist cried at leaving her painting at my house. We would all weep every day if we could see so clearly that yesterday's efforts do not preclude tomorrow's labor. Inevitably, no matter how tired we are, we must stand up and start a new picture, the one that, like a full moon, will pull us along through the human night.

ABOUT THE AUTHOR

Susan Carol Hauser is an essayist, poet, and freelance writer. She has an MFA in poetry from Bowling Green State University in Ohio and an MA in English from Northern Michigan University at Marquette. Her essay collections include *Meant to Be Read Out Loud* (Loonfeather Press, 1988), recipient of a 1989 Minnesota Book Award; *Girl to Woman* (Astarte Shell Press, 1992); and *Which Way to Look* (Loonfeather Press, 1992). She has written a poetry collection, *Redpoll on a Broken Branch* (Same Name Press, 1992), and has been published in numerous anthologies, including *Eating Our Hearts Out* (The Crossing Press, 1993) and *I Am Becoming the Woman I've Wanted* (Papier-Mache Press, 1994). Her recent book, *Nature's Revenge* (Lyons & Burford, 1996), is a natural history of poison ivy, poison oak, and poison sumac. Her radio script, *Loss into Light: Emerging from the Darkness That Is Grief*, with music by Mary Clemenson, received a 1992–93 Gabrielle Award for excellence in radio broadcast, and she is a commentator on the Minnesota Public Radio network. Recipient of a 1994 Minnesota Governor's Award for Leadership, she lives in rural northern Minnesota.

PAPIER-MACHE PRESS

At Papier-Mache Press, it is our goal to identify and successfully present important social issues through enduring works of beauty, grace, and strength. Through our work we hope to encourage empathy and respect among diverse communities, creating a bridge of understanding between the mainstream audience and those who might not otherwise be heard.

We appreciate you, our customer, and strive to earn your continued support. We also value the role of the bookseller in achieving our goals. We are especially grateful to the many independent booksellers whose presence ensures a continuing diversity of opinion, information, and literature in our communities. We encourage you to support these bookstores with your patronage.

We publish many fine books about women's experiences. We also produce lovely posters and T-shirts that complement our anthologies. Please ask your local bookstore which Papier-Mache items they carry. To receive our complete catalog, send your request to Papier-Mache Press, 135 Aviation Way, #14, Watsonville, CA 95076, or call our toll-free number, 800-927-5913.